ARAK AND MEZZE

To General George Bitar (1923-2007) a gentleman, a
champion soldier and one of Lebanon's finest Arak makers

Arak and Mezze

The Taste of Lebanon

Michael Karam | Photographs by Norbert Schiller

SAQI

ISBN 13: 978-0-86356-476-5

Text copyright © Michael Karam, 2008
Photography copyright © Norbert Schiller, 2008
Additional photographic credits: p. 2: George Bitar family collection; p. 25: Michael Karam; pp. 48, 153: Tanail Jesuit Monastery collection; pp. 51, 75: Touma family collection; p. 66: Domaine des Tourelles collection

A full CIP record for this book is available from the British Library
A full CIP record for this book is available from the Library of Congress

Designed by: Marya Cheaib
Manufactured in Lebanon by: Chemaly & Chemaly

SAQI
26 Westbourne Grove, London W2 5RH
825 Page Street, Suite 203, Berkeley, California 94710
Tabet Building, Mneimneh Street, Hamra, Beirut
www.saqibooks.com

Contents

'Arak, the local aperitif, is very good; made from a grape basis and flavoured with aniseed, it is vaguely reminiscent of Pernod, and has, further, the advantage of being something of a specific against the intestinal troubles which so commonly beset the traveler in the Middle East.'

Robin Fedden, *Syria and Lebanon: An Historical Appreciation*

'I trusted in the hospitality of the ahl al-Jabal, the people of the mountain.'

Colin Thubron, *The Hills of Adonis*

'I asked your grandfather why he drank three glasses of arak every day: one in the morning, one at noon and one at night. "It's medicine young man," he barked. He was right. Soon after that, I went to see a friend in hospital who told me that the doctor had said he could drink a little arak. What happened to him? Oh, he died later that week, but it wasn't the arak!'

Elias Karam, seventy-five, farmer and arak maker
Conversation with the author August, 2006

'What is arak to me? My son, it is life. It is the lion's milk; it is the Virgin's tear.'

Ibid

Acknowledgments

The authors would like to give special thanks to Elias Fadel and his staff for their time, patience and enthusiasm in preparing the mezze dishes and allowing the premises to used for photo shoots; Rula Karam for her magic recipes; Ramzi and Sami Ghosn for their tireless support and advice; Me Charles Ghostine, Khalil Sara and Michel Shalhoub, all of whom facilitated the trip to Hina; Joane Issa and Dana Smilie for their photographic input and finally Anissa Rafeh for her expert handling of an ice cream cone.

They would also like to thank Dr Carlos Adem; Michel de Bustros; Tanios Fahed; Serge and Ronald Hochar; Eli, Christiane and Fawzi Issa; Captain Habib Karam; Georges Kazzan; Nayla and Emile Issa el Khoury; Emile Majdalani, Bassam, Sami, Samir and Salim Naked; Sayeed, Assad, and Nathalie and Micheline Touma; Walid Touma; Dargham Touma; Rania Chammas; Paulette Chlela and Hanna Daou.

Finally, they would like to acknowledge the good people of Zabougha, in particular Elias Karam, Sami Kerbage, Joseph Qai, and George Haibeh.

What is Lebanon?

Lebanon is situated at the eastern extremity of the Mediterranean. With a population of four million, it is bordered by Syria to the north and the east and Israel to the south. It is also the site of Phoenicia, one of the world's oldest civilizations, which bequeathed modern Lebanon some of the most magnificently preserved ruins from antiquity.

Lebanon is also a crucible of the three great monotheist religions – Christianity, Islam and Judaism – and is home to eighteen state-recognized faiths. This consensus is reflected in the constitution, which in 1943, the year Lebanon became an independent nation, distributed political representation according to this confessional dynamic and its demographic spread. Today, based on an admittedly outdated 1932 census, the president is drawn from the ranks of the Maronite Christian community, the speaker of parliament is a Shia Muslim and the prime minister a Sunni Muslim. Other religious communities – Greek Orthodox, Druze, Greek Catholic, Armenian Catholic, Protestant – are also represented.

The years following Lebanon's independence allowed the country to thrive while other nations in the region struggled to cope with the twin ructions of the creation of the state of Israel and the phenomenon of Arab nationalism. It styled itself a regional refuge for bankers, émigrés, diplomats, spies, traders and the like, acquiring along the way a patina of sophistication and intrigue.

But patina it was. The lead-up to the 1975–90 civil war revealed a flaw in Lebanon's proud multi-confessional make-up as the country was forced to take sides in an ever-widening struggle against Israel. It became a country divided. War brought with it mass immigration, infrastructural destruction, confessional suspicion and volcanic inflation.

In 1989, Lebanon lurched, punch-drunk, into a peace process that saw significant constitutional adjustments that were designed to end the war,

Facing page: Hiking in the Qadisha valley

which eventually ended in October 1990. Seventeen years on, Lebanon has succeeded in rescuing some of its pre-war glamour, even if it is still affected by the tiresome realities of the region and periods of instability.

But Lebanon is more than just politics and conflict. It is a country with rippling, snow-capped mountains that rise steeply off the coast, deep, deep valleys and ports that once served as the commercial hub of the civilized world.

It is a country where waiters speak three languages and where secretaries dress like film stars. Its doctors are among the best in the region and its engineers can lay credible claim to have built the modern Gulf nations. It singers and musicians are fêted around the Arab world, while many of its writers have gained prominence in languages other than Arabic. Among the Arab nations, it has the best food, wine and arak, the best schools and the freest press.

It should be one of the most dynamic countries in the world. And yet it remains an intriguing contradiction: a pleasure dome for vacationing Gulf Arabs who come for the liberal milieu, the three-million dollar penthouses and the beautiful women, it is nonetheless an emerging economy with a creaking infrastructure and an outmoded political class. At all times though, it remains a beacon for coexistence in the Middle East and the world at large.

Sunday strollers in the newly renovated Beirut Central District or Downtown

Facing page: Hot summer night in Gemmayzeh: the Lebanese have a thirst for going out and having fun

Following page: Modern Beirut is still a vibrant contrast of old and new

Lebanon: The Vine and Wine

The Phoenicians, a Semitic people whose hubs were the ancient cities of Byblos, Sidon and Tyre, began making and exporting their wine around 3000 BC. Their passion for viticulture grew out of necessity. Land in these city-states was scarce and it made commercial sense to grow grapes, the produce from which could be exchanged for crops that required more arable land. In this way, one of the first great viticultural communities emerged. At the height of their commercial dominance between 900 and 330 BC, the Phoenicians' all-powerful trading fleets carried their wines throughout the Mediterranean to Egypt, Carthage, Cyprus, Greece, Ancient Rome, Sardinia and Spain. They also sailed beyond the Straits of Gibraltar to France and as far north as Cornwall on the southwest coast of England.

But wine-making in Lebanon can be traced back to before the Phoenician era. It is generally accepted that what is now Lebanon was, possibly as far back as 7000 BC, home to some of the very earliest wine-making, falling as it does within the rough triangle that takes in the Caucasus (modern Armenia and Georgia) to the north, Mesopotamia (modern Iraq) to the east and southern Palestine to the west. It is in this area that wine historians believe that the first wines were made around 8000 BC.

There is the story of Noah, captain of the ark, who, after the flood, it is said in the Bible, became the first *vigneron*. The Book of Genesis goes on to tell us the effect wine had on him: 'Noah began to be a husbandman, and he planted a vineyard. And he drank of the wine, and was drunken; and he was uncovered within his tent.'

Did Noah's ark alight, as many people claim, on Lebanon's Mount Sannine rather than Mount Ararat, in the Taurus Mountains on the Turkish-Armenian border? Could it be his tomb in the mosque at Kerak, a village just outside Zahleh and a stone's throw from Château Ksara? If so, did Noah

Facing page: A dedication to the Roman gods in the Bekaa town of Qab Elias

Following page: The Crusader sea fort in Sidon

17

husband his grapes in the Bekaa and did early viticulture reach the area through his reputation as a viticulturalist? It's a good story.

And then, of course, there is the supposed relationship with Bacchus, the Roman god of wine, to whom the awesome temple in Baalbek is said to be dedicated. Built in the middle of the second century AD, it is the best-preserved Roman temple anywhere in the world. It is believed that local fertility cults, whose worship revolved around the idea of resurrection – expressed initially through the agricultural cycle of sowing, growing, harvesting and feasting – came to idolize Bacchus with a wine-based ritual.

Bacchus is believed to figure on two reliefs carved around the entrance to the temple. Today, these carvings have been badly eroded, but one shows the birth of Bacchus, coming from the thigh of his father Zeus, and the other a group of revellers, one of whom is said to be Bacchus, apparently leaning on a vine and holding an ancient goblet made from animal horn.

The story of Bacchus is nothing more than that – a legend. But what we do know is that the bartering Phoenicians (and perhaps even returning French Crusaders) played a major role in giving Lebanon's wine to the world, and from this evolved the culture of the grape and, of course, arak.

The Temple of Bacchus in Baalbek in the Bekaa

Facing page: The entrance to the temple

Following page: The harbour of the ancient city of Byblos

Arak and Mezze

The Tao of Arak –
A Personal Journey

Origins

This book is particularly important to me because I come from the mountains of Lebanon, home to the arak tradition. The fact that I was born in London is merely a byproduct of the Lebanese millennia-old urge to travel, not unlike the impact made by arak over ten centuries and two continents.

It is a story that we can pick up at the end of the nineteenth century, when, like many Lebanese at the time, my grandfather, Esper Karam, left his mountain village of Zabougha and headed for Brazil, presumably to improve his chances of getting on in life. There, in the best Lebanese tradition, he established Esperadio Karam Trading and, by all accounts, prospered. He became a senior freemason in the Sao Paulo lodge, learnt Portuguese and married a Swedish woman.

In 1915, he returned to Lebanon with his young family, just in time to be caught in the blockade of Beirut and the ensuing famine. In Zabougha the people starved, with many resorting to eating radishes and even grass to survive. My Swedish grandmother took in needy children, children who would otherwise have died, cared for them and returned them to their families when things improved.

Esper still had the Lebanese pioneering spirit surging through his veins and, unable to sit still, he headed off to Mali, where, with his brother Salim, he established another trading concern in Koulikoro. Working in Mali today would be no picnic; quite what it was like in the 1920s is unimaginable. But the heat, the malaria and the ever-present threat of violence did not deter a man who, despite his habit of losing money at cards, was not afraid of hard work.

And he worked hard enough to bring up six children, one of whom, my father, joined Lebanon's national carrier, Middle East Airlines, and was posted to London, where I was born in 1965, a year after Esper Karam passed away at the age of eighty-six. He drank three glasses of arak each day, one at breakfast, one at lunchtime and one in the evening. He claimed it was his medicine.

So, by a twist of fate a son of the Lebanese mountains ended up living and growing up in Kensington, going to prep school in the genteel Surrey town of Haslemere and public school in Petworth, West Sussex.

Esper Karam, the author's grandfather, who is understood to have drunk three glasses of arak each day: one in the morning, one at noon and one in the evening

Childhood

School holidays before the 1975 Lebanon civil war were spent in Lebanon. I was too young to fully enjoy the fleshy delights of pre-war Beirut, but Zabougha proved a Narnia-like wonderland for a little boy whisked over from an England of school blazers, pillow fights, conkers and under-10 cricket matches. The village was still very primitive. Many of the homes had no bathrooms or toilets and our house had one of two televisions in the village. Apart from the weekly episode of *Kojak*, we got our kicks from banging percussion caps with a stone, hurling firecrackers at unsuspecting nuns, making catapults, riding hoops and seeing who could throw rocks the furthest, an eccentric test of manliness in mountain life. The highlight of the week was arguably the arrival of the neighbourhood ice cream van driven by Mr Toufic. Twenty-five piasters bought you one scoop, but, being the indulged son of a well-to-do *khawaja* (gentleman), I enjoyed two scoops with the half-lira coin my unmarried, paternal aunt Selma retrieved from her purse and slipped into my hand after breakfast.

Zabougha lived off the land. Much of my time was spent either picking grapes and figs for Selma, being told to avoid treading on her sumac fruit drying on blankets in the baking sun, watching her make *kaak il eid* (a round biscuit made during religious celebrations) or sitting with the women of the village as they cheerfully sat around the ovens baking *marqouq* (very thin Arabic bread).

Grapes meant arak, the clear drink that looked like water and smelt like liquorice. I knew the aroma from the unmarked bottle in my parent's drinks cabinet in London, but Zabougha was the mother ship. The men were always drinking arak from small glasses at all times of day and if they weren't drinking it they were talking about how, when and where they would make it. There were ten stills in the village, but I had always returned to England before they 'removed' the arak. It was obviously one of the highlights of the years and I felt I was missing out.

Facing page: Grapes play an important part in Lebanese village life

Loss

In the summer of 1974, my father indulged me further, arranging for me to have a donkey. The next day a very old man, ramrod straight, turbaned and dressed in the *sherwal* (traditional black baggy trousers) delivered a splendid black animal to our house on the condition I return it at the end of each day. This I did, and I came to befriend the man, who told me that every evening before going to sleep he would treat himself to a handful of pistachio nuts washed down with a glass of arak. He would then repeat the Lebanese adage, *Neym bakeer, qum baker. Shoof il sahat keef betseer* (Sleep early and rise early and you will see how healthy you become), cross himself and close his eyes.

One day, I went as usual to collect my donkey only to find a group of people gathered outside his modest two-room, single-storey house. I pushed through into the main room and walked over to his bed in the corner. He was dead, and had already been laid out, his arms crossed under his white face. Next to him on the bedside table lay the pistachio shells and the empty arak glass.

Later that morning, I watched the young men of the village make space in the *abr*, or tomb, and looked on in open-mouthed amazement as they casually stacked the skulls of the earlier incumbents on a rocky shelf at the back of the vault.

With the arrival of war, the holidays in Zabougha dried up, as did my interest in my Lebanese roots. In 1990, the year the war would eventually end, my father died in an air crash in Sierra Leone. It was decided that we should bring his body back to the village. Zabougha was exactly as I remembered it. My childhood friends were still there (although Toufic, the ice cream man, had died) and we reconnected with remarkable ease despite the fifteen-year absence.

The night before we buried my father, we held a wake in the main dining room. Lebanon was still at war; electricity was haphazard and paint was peeling from the ceiling. As my father lay in the next room, family members who had not seen each other in over ten years, divided by either

Facing page: Georges Haibeh tending to his still in Zabougha

war or forced emigration, gathered round the huge dining table my father had shipped over from London years earlier. I remember it as a happy affair despite the sudden and tragic circumstances that brought us together. My uncle, whom I had not seen for ten years, passed me an arak, telling me that, as I was from the mountains, I should be drinking a real mountain drink. As I put the glass to my nostrils, the familiar childhood smell of aniseed came racing back. The next day we slid his coffin into the same tomb I had helped tidy all those years ago, and I realized that one day I too would be carried the short way from St Georges Church, up the steps, to lie among the bones of my ancestors.

The harvest is a happy and carefree rural tradition. The heartbeat of agricultural Lebanon

Facing page: George Kazzan holds up arak, bottled the year he was born

Arak and Mezze

Alchemy

A year later, I found myself at a house party in Cherbourg on the west coast of France. My host had offered me a glass of pastis and, sitting on his verandah looking out across the channel, I told him about Lebanon and a similar drink called arak. 'Of course, the Arabs gave it to us,' he said, 'but I'm sure you know that,' he added politely. I mumbled something and nodded, but the truth was I didn't. Why should a twenty-five-year-old man brought up in England appreciate the fact that in the sixth century Jaber Ibn Hayyan, a Muslim chemist, invented the still and perfected the process of distillation, primarily to make *al-kouhoul,* the black eye make-up from which the word alcohol is derived?

Why should I have cared that by the ninth century, *arak* (literally 'the sweat or the juice') had spread to what is now Iraq, Egypt and Iran? Should I have fussed that by the eleventh century, the distillation process had reached Europe by way of Moorish Spain and inspired the great *eau de vie* of the Mediterranean basin such as ouzo (Greece), mastika (Macedonia), raki (Turkey), pastis (France), sambuca (Italy) and ojén (Spain)?

Did it really matter that, while the drink was making its way across Europe courtesy of Arab scholars, the caravans heading east also made their mark on the cultures they encountered and that today the word *arak* describes other *eau de vie* as far away as China and Indonesia as well in Korea, where it is known as *soju*?

At the time, no, it didn't.

Return

I moved to Lebanon in February 1992 and immediately commandeered my late father's car – a huge 1977 Buick Electra – from a cousin who, judging by the overpowering aroma of aniseed, had been using it to ferry around his homemade arak. If ever I was going to be converted to Lebanon's national drink this was not the way to do it. In any case, whisky was the tipple of choice

for Lebanese who wanted to put on a show. Dewar's White Label ensured it was king among Lebanese drinkers, primarily by blitzing the nation's TVs and billboards with a huge media campaign and the legend 'When it's love, it never varies'. The TV commercials were unabashedly mushy vehicles for overplayed love ballads such as Nilsson's 'Without you' and Shirley Bassey's 'Impossible', but for a nation stumbling into the daylight after years of civil war darkness, they were a welcome diversion.

It also meant that bottles of Dewar's, the equally popular J&B (whose more risqué advertising featured unconventional newly-weds in the Nevada desert with handcuffs, pinball machine and a bottle of whisky) and Johnny Walker Black Label – the enduringly popular choice of the more affluent tippler – were omnipresent on every dining table. Nothing else would do and to hell with etiquette. The Lebanese had fifteen years of catching up to do and they wanted to do it with whisky. Wine, they complained, especially Lebanese wine, gave them a headache, while arak was quite simply a peasant drink.

A family affair: commercial airline pilot, Captain Habib Karam and Lisa, his children's nanny, strive to make the perfect arak

Awakening

I had my first real arak-with-food experience over a hearty breakfast in 1999 with Andrew Harvey, my editor at the *Beirut Daily Star*. It was a slow morning at the paper, so we slipped off down the road to Le Chef, the celebrated eatery on Rue Gouraud, Gemayzeh's main thoroughfare, where we ordered *bayd awarma* (eggs fried in fat-laden mince) and then decided that it would be a naughty wheeze to drink some arak with our artery-crushing food. Three miniatures of Ksarak later, I found myself walking back to work suitably refreshed and nonetheless thrilled by fact that here was a tipple that was OK to drink at breakfast without being labelled a functional alcoholic.

Months later, I went to my butcher in Kfaraqab, the village next to Zabougha. It was 8.00 AM on a November morning. The butcher in his bloodstained apron, who had been up since four, was standing at his counter, finishing a breakfast of *kibbe nayeh* (raw, puréed minced meat), blended with herbs and covered with olive oil. On a side dish were chunks of raw liver and a few pieces of fat. He made a scoop with the bread and rounded up meat, fat and oil and washed it down with a glass of arak. He offered me a glass with the last pieces of raw purée. My conversion was complete. To hell with the whisky-slugging bourgeois of Beirut; this was Lebanon.

The next month, Andrew came into the newsroom with two beautiful slim blue bottles he was taking as Christmas gifts to friends in London. Arak Massaya had been on the local market for a few years and their distinctive blue bottles had begun to make an impact. Not only was this an attractive product that was also Lebanese, but what was inside didn't taste bad either. More and more people offered Massaya arak as gifts: the idea that arak really could be cool began, like a creeping vine, to wrap itself round the Lebanese consciousness. Massaya owners Sami and Ramzi Ghosn certainly never doubted it would, and had started a revolution that would reshape the map of the Lebanese wine and arak sector.

Facing page: A global brand: Massaya leads the way in making arak sexy

Serendipity

Four years later, I was the Lebanon correspondent for Tom Stevenson's *Wine Report*. The Ghosns had become friends, and it was at a lunch at Massaya in September 2003 that I met the photographer Norbert Schiller; he was working with Max Rodenbeck of the *Economist*, who was researching what would be a thrilling and inspirational story on arak for the Christmas 2003 issue.

Norbert spent lunch talking ad nauseam about his dream to buy a microbrewery, a subject that Ramzi Ghosn felt verged on blasphemy as we sat among the vines during harvest. As lunch broke up, it was obvious Norbert was still thirsty. Nudging me, he asked in a whisper if it would be OK if we cracked into the unopened, and until now ignored, bottle of arak sitting in the middle of the table. Until that moment I had been happy to finish my lunchtime imbibing, but Norbert's question prompted one of those rare but refreshing moments when you just say 'hell, why not?' Here was a man, who has since told me on many occasions that life is serious enough when you are having fun so why cut it out when you don't need to. It was a beginning. Two years later Norbert and I had our first book published, *Wines of Lebanon*.

In doing so, we had caught the arak bug, for all the wine makers were also arak producers. Some had always made arak and had branched into wine – Clos St Thomas, Wardy and Massaya – while others – Château Musar, Château Ksara, Château Kefraya and Vin Nakad – made arak as a sideline, making good use of the sub-standard grapes.

And then there was Le Brun.

There was a time – during the civil war and just after – when, if whisky wasn't your thing and you insisted on drinking arak and keeping up appearances, it had to be Le Brun.

Created by a Pierre Brun, a third-generation immigrant from France, arak Le Brun was hailed as Lebanon's finest. Brun died in 2000, and the company was taken over by Elie Issa, a former Lebanese judo champion who competed in the 1976 Montréal Olympics and who had been a close friend

Facing page: The tomb of
Pierre Brun in Jdeita

of Brun. I got to know Elie while writing *Wines of Lebanon*; and when Saqi agreed to publish this book, I asked him, as we searched for the Brun family vault in a rain-drenched churchyard in the Bekaa town of Jdeita, where he bought his aniseed.

'Go to Hina, in the foothills of Jabel El Shiekh (Mount Hermon),' he said, 'Ah, here he is,' he exclaimed as Norbert and I navigated between the withered crucifixes. 'This is where they put Pierre.'

Il Balad ll Sham

'Elie is correct,' confirmed Charles Ghostine, the managing director of Château Ksara. 'The best aniseed must come from Hina. It is a military zone, but if you go with our agent in Syria it should not be a problem. I will arrange it.'

It had seemed like a good place to start on the book, and so it came to pass that I was sitting in Ali's white Volvo as he drove hell for leather, all windows down, for the Syrian border. He certainly knew the road, but this still didn't stop me gripping the handle above the door, both knuckles white. 'Perhaps it's because he does the run several times a day and the faster the turn-around the faster he can get home to Mrs Ali,' screamed Lee Smith, the American writer with whom I was travelling. 'Maybe?'

The mountain resorts of Bhamdoun and Sofar whizzed by as we descended into Chtaura, the gateway to the Bekaa valley, and hurtled first past the Jesuit monastery at Tanail, site of the genesis of Lebanon's modern wine industry, and then the elegant signs for Massaya, old and new flanking the way to Syria and the biblical foothills of Jabal El Sheikh and the aniseed fields of Hina.

Aniseed sifting at harvest
time in Hina

Hina

I wondered what the mood would be like in Damascus. Would I feel the trauma that Syria had endured six months earlier when, after nearly thirty years of 'occupation', its army had been forced to withdraw from Lebanon in the wake of the assassination of ex-prime minister Rafic Hariri and twenty-two others in a huge explosion on the seafront in front of the famous St George's Hotel?

It was a quiet day at the border, and soon we were screaming past the wind-blown trees on the highway into Damascus, where Norbert was waiting at the Sheraton Hotel and where we met Michel Shalhoub, Château Ksara's contact. He was driving a tiny Mazda that, like my father's Buick, also reeked of aniseed. 'Jump in,' he said cheerily, 'but please, cameras in the boot. We are going to an army area.'

We drove on out of Damascus and headed in the direction of Israel, sharing the rutted roads with baby-laden mothers riding side-saddle on groaning mopeds, belching tractors and the odd donkey cart, all of which were occasionally scattered by enormous juggernauts that appeared out of the shimmering heat.

Keeping in lane was obviously optional and suddenly Beirut – my usual acme for motoring madness – seemed like Zurich. Like Ali, the chain-smoking Mr Shalhoub drove, also with the windows down, as if his wife were about to give birth. He told us that the Shalhoubs have been making arak since 1954. 'Yes, the Turks make raki and Greeks make ouzo, but the aniseed is too big and does not give enough flavour.' Michel also told us that we were going to the village of Kanaker, to the see the *gherbal* (the industrial sifter used to process the aniseed).

Does he want to talk politics? Why not? 'It was a big blow for us to leave Lebanon.' His words are almost lost in the howl of the wind. The car has no air conditioning and the back of my shirt is drenched. 'We felt it hard,' he screams even louder. Judging by the defeated looks on their faces, the Syrian people seem to be feeling a lot of things hard as they watch us drive by.

We pass the first army checkpoint, which is unmanned. Michel points to a road heading west and a mountain looming ahead. 'That is *jabal el sheikh*. You can see the Israeli telescope on the top. They can see everything, even us in this car! Do you know why it is called *jabal el sheikh*? It is because the snow on the top never melted and looked like a sheikh's headdress.' He pauses. 'That was about until about ten years ago. Now the world is hotter. What can you do? Everything is changing.'

Kanaker, at an altitude of 600 metres, is a poor village, and Michel, a Christian, was at pains to tell me it is Muslim. The houses are made of undressed breeze block, although there appears to be enough money in each home for the dozens of satellite dishes that decorate the village. School kids mill around.

The *gherbal* has seen better days. Outside sit two goats, shaded from the heat as Mohammed oversees the entire sifting process. This may not be his name. When I asked Michel, he shrugged, 'I don't know. Just call him Mohammed.' Michel buys 16 tons of aniseed each year, ten of which go to Château Ksara for its famous Ksarak, and the rest is used by his family's company.

The air is thick with green dust as the machine swallows the seed (*Pimpinella anisum*) and throws it up on the sieve, spitting it into sacks. Mohammed might have to do it four or five times to achieve the purest seeds.

Sneezing, we drove back to Kanaker and headed for Hina, through an area that, Michel tells us, is predominantly Druze and Christian, although Hina (population 10,000) is entirely Christian. Like Kanaker, the place is awash with schoolchildren. Their uniforms are smarter, with a more Western cut and made of drill cotton. A girl, probably no older than seventeen, walked past, coyly glancing at the two foreigners, or *ajaneb*.

'Yes of course,' answers Michel when I tentatively ask him if, as I sense, there is a feeling of rural happiness. 'There is no stress like we feel in the city. Here they sow, grow and reap. What can be better than that?' Quite.

Michel admitted he is fanatical about buying his aniseed. He stabbed the bags with his *allam* (literally a pen, and which does indeed look like a giant nib). It is in fact a scoop, and with it he can check the quality of the seeds, which are then sent to the *gherbal* where they are sifted (losing 30 per cent in the process) and then returned to Hina, where they are sifted one last time with the all the

Facing page: Mohammed emptying a bag of Aniseed for further sifting

bags to achieve a kind of uniformity. Michel watches the whole process with lynx-like resolve. 'Once it gets to the market, who knows what is in it,' he asks soberly. 'Many people will tell you they are selling aniseed from Hina, but it could be mixed with stuff from fields at the lower levels. Hina's annual crop of 200 tons of aniseed is the best because it doesn't have much dew, which is why it retains most of the perfume. There is none purer than this.'

Transition

Back in Beirut it is a quiet and overcast morning on Rue Gouraud, an area that until five years ago was a sleepy lower-middle class neighbourhood with not much going for it apart from the ever-full Le Chef, the picturesque St Nicholas steps, a café where men play *tawleh* (an Ottoman version of backgammon) and a printing press owned by the Misrahis, one of Beirut's few surviving Jewish families. There were also the offices of Arak Kazzan,

The best in the world: Mohammed holds a handful of purity

an obscure brand, whose corporate livery hints at a more prosperous past. Norbert and I take a glance inside, to be confronted with a desk piled high with Dickensian book-keeping paraphernalia and the whiff of another age. George Kazzan, bearded and natty in lightweight but distressed tweeds, is sitting inside with an air of resignation.

Gemayzeh is undergoing a seismic gentrification; the printers have gone, giving way to what will be the first of many bars and clubs that will come and go along the bustling strip – Kazzan is next to go, bought out. It is the end of an era. George Kazzan holds up a dusty bottle of arak made the year he was born. 'What can I say?' he shrugs. 'Beirut is changing; Lebanon is changing; the world is changing.'

Hope

Tanail, May 2007. It is my birthday and the second Massaya arak 'workshop', a family day out at which one can make one's own arak. Yes, the Ghosns are building up a head of steam with arak culture, fighting a valiant rearguard action to champion this wonderful drink.

I am nursing a mild hangover, having been to an office party at Element,

End of an era: Arak Kazzan moves out of its original premises in Gemayzeh to make way for a cocktail bar. Owner George Kazzan (left), and his friends face the end with stoicism and a bit of humour

one of Beirut's most chichi clubs, where amid the din of Bruce Springsteen (it was *that* kind of age group) I asked the barman for an arak. He looked at me at first surprised and then nodded approvingly, returning with a huge tumbler of white liquid garnished with a sprig of mint. The two men between whom I had barged to order my drink took one look at my arak and ordered one each.

I tell this to a happy Ramzi Ghosn as the visitors queue to pay and receive their complimentary Arak Massaya bandana and mark out their positions among the rugs, hay bales and wooden chairs. On a public holiday the brothers have succeeded in dragging a sizeable chunk of Lebanon's *jeunesse dorée* (including, I learn later, the staff of Element who chose Massaya for their 'office' day-out) across into the Bekaa for an arakfest.

Lebanon is finding a happy middle ground. The Lebanese now recognize that embracing the rural past can be done with pride and a sense of fun. Try telling a Scotsman he should not be proud of his whisky – in fact, try telling the Scottish tourist board that whisky should be removed as one of it main attractions.

Where does arak go from here? It is a national jewel that should be polished. A law should be passed in which the strictest guidelines (see 'The perfect arak') for the production of authentic arak should be laid down. Let those who still want to make 'ordinary' arak do so, but let there be a benchmark for a premium product that, like wine, will take the best of Lebanon to the world. The Scots did it with malt and premium whisky and the Mexicans did it with tequila.

The El Dorado is, of course, arak as a global brand. There is no reason this should not happen, if the massive drinks distributors deem it so. If tequila, which came out of Mexico via the frat houses and cocktail bars of the United States, can delight tipplers across the world, then arak with all its glorious history and its proven purity can do so too. Lebanese food has been in the international consciousness much longer than sushi, but somehow we all know of sake; why not arak? It has not been tarnished as a tourist cliché like sangria or ouzo and can be marketed as the drink that started it all. There could even be an arak museum in the Bekaa.

It's just an idea.

Facing page: Arak al fresco in the Bekaa

Following page: Making grape alcohol the traditional way at the monastery in Bzummar

Arak: A Brief History

Until the mid-twentieth century, arak was the drink of choice for the rich. If you drank arak, you owned a *karakeh* (a still) or at the very least had access to one. If you didn't, you made wine, which was easier and cheaper to produce. This snobbery would be inverted in the mid-1990s when arak producers such as Touma and Ghantous Abu Raad rushed to join in the new global wine revolution. By that time, Lebanon had become more industrialized and arak had become more freely available. It had lost its cachet and been usurped by whisky.

But before that, before Lebanon began to feel the ripples of the industrial revolution, around the turn of the twentieth century, very few farmers could afford a still. Up until that point, arak was the drink of the upper classes. The *bey*, *basha* or the *khawajah* would have his still; it would be a sign of rank. He would distribute arak to his favoured tenant farmers as an annual bonus, and this would represent the farmer's *mouni* (his arak supply) for the season. Alternatively, a *vigneron* might ask his landlord for the use of his still to make arak, offering him in return a share of the final produce, a quid pro quo that still exists. A nabob from a long-standing North Lebanon family complained recently that these days he was forced to distribute smaller quantities of arak and that this had presented him in a poor light, but what could he do?

Industrialization changed all that. The smith and his copper were everywhere, and stills became more affordable. There was a stampede to own one and elevate one's standing (it mattered not that the *basha* had now probably bought his first car and the whole system had shunted along one notch). When people said *bidi sheel ara'ti* (I want to make my arak), what in effect they were saying was that they were rich enough to have a still. Even now a mountain host might show his guests his still as part of the 'let me show you around' tour.

The upshot of the availability of the still was an explosion in the arak

Facing page: Harvesting grapes at Tanail in the Bekaa in the 1940s

49

market in the 50s and 60s, and, like all good Lebanese, many entrepreneurs saw an opportunity. One famous businessman went to Russia and bought a still that could make arak not just from grapes but from potatoes and beetroot. The Lebanese state had other more pressing matters at hand than to take an interest in enforcing the arak law, and the new breed of industrial producers could now make arak at a fraction of the price; the Lebanese consumer, always happy to feel he is getting a bargain, snapped it up. OK, it wasn't made with the Obeideh or the Merweh grape, but it was, they reasoned, arak. What they didn't know, or possibly even care about, was that the reputation of arak was going into a nosedive.

With the war the genuine arak maker could not compete. Ghantous Abou Raad was king while Touma was selling his produce to a thirsty Iraqi market. Only Le Brun, who was situated on the main Damascus road in Chtaura and who was protected by the local authorities, was able to smuggle his arak to the Christian areas, where, along with newly released Ksarak by Château Ksara, it became the only acceptable label.

The wine producers made arak as sub-businesses, a way to make good use of inferior grapes. Noel Rabot, Ksara's winemaker from 1974 to 1992 explains the philosophy. 'Ksara's development may have been frozen in its tracks by the war, but what did advance, slowly but surely, despite everything, was the production of arak. One of the great advantages of the Ksara winery was that we could keep the good wines and get rid of those we didn't like. If only I could do the same thing in France. At Ksara, I didn't have to sit around saying "this isn't good, what am I going to do with it?" If I didn't like it, I sent it to the distillery, because we needed wine alcohol for the arak.'

Massaya in its sexy bottle changed the arak dynamic. It was lifted out of rural obscurity and made urbane and elegant, restored it to its rightful position at the forefront of the Lebanese culinary tradition. 'I would like to think we gave the sector a new perspective,' says Massaya's Ramzi Ghosn. 'We said we are going to make good arak the proper way, the traditional way. We felt the Lebanese needed reminding that when they eat mezze they must drink arak to respect their food. Arak is part of our past and it can also be our future.'

Facing page: Arak Touma is one of Lebanese oldest and most famous tipples. An early shot of one of the current owners, Sayeed Touma, proudly showing off the company transport

Following page: Ramzi Ghosn, who with his brother Sami took arak from rural moonshine to sophisticated eau de vie

The Angel's Share

The arak production process begins with the grapes. For our purposes they should be white Lebanese varietals, preferably Obeideh or Merweh (although Ugni Blanc, the preferred grape in the Cognac region of France, can also be used). The Obeideh should be crushed slowly and allowed to ferment naturally without the addition of artificial yeasts.

The wine alcohol level should reach around 13 per cent before the first distillation process or *brouillis* (literally the first draft). The still's head should be an Arab head or *tête de maure* (moor's head) – unlike other stills such as the swan's head or the rectification column, the Arab head exerts less pressure and is more gentle in extracting the aniseed aromas with the distillate. It should also be made of copper, which has the best properties with which to manipulate 70 per cent alcohol, being malleable and a good conductor of heat. It resists corrosion from fire and from wine and reacts well with wine components such as sulphur and fatty acids.

The fire under the still should be lit with vine wood. Not only does this guarantee that no chemicals enter the production process, it ensures that none of the raw materials in the production process goes to waste. Heat is evenly distributed to avoid any build-up of charring in the still and also creates the sense of ritual essential to the perpetuity of any national tradition.

The output should then be allowed to sit for one to two months before the second distillation, during which the distillate is divided into the head, the heart and the tail. The head – the aromas of which are too aggressive – and the tail – with the aromas too dull – are removed, leaving only the *coeur* (the heart), which has the right balance. In this way the harmful methanol and other ingredients are removed. The new, purer distillate is left to sit for another one to two months before the third and final distillation, which sees

Facing page: The arak must then be aged in clay jars. The best are made in mountain town of Beit Shabeb just outside Beirut, where it is said that the clay in the soil offers the best porosity. The ageing process is important for it allows for the evaporation of the low density alcoholic properties (the parts that can cause a hangover). This evaporation –roughly 5 percent – is known affectionately in the distillation process as the Angel's share.

the addition of the fresh aniseed that must come from the Syrian village of Hina (see page 40). The aniseed should not be more than one season old.

The output undergoes a further separation of the head and the tail from the now ultra-pure heart. The arak has now been broken down into its purest form (there is a myth that a fourth or even fifth stage can achieve a purer state, but this is nothing more than a one-upmanship gimmick: in fact, the more times you distill, the more of the aroma you lose).

The arak must then be aged in clay jars. The best are made in the mountain town of Beit Shabeb just outside Beirut, where it is said that the clay in the soil offers the best porosity. The ageing process is important, since it allows for the evaporation of the low-density alcoholic properties (the parts that cause hangovers). This evaporation – roughly 5 per cent – is known affectionately in the distillation process as the Angel's share.

All arak makers agree, however, that it must be made with passion. Human intervention is crucial to making a good arak. Let then the intervention be made with the hand of a patient craftsman.

Previous pages: (Left): These two 500-lb stills being loaded onto the truck in the northern port of Tripoli are destined for Massaya. Ramzi Ghosn chose the traditional still-making techniques of Lebanon's second biggest city as a part of his brand's commitment to using only the best traditional methods to make his arak. As with most removal situations in Lebanon, the logistics of getting it out of the workshop and onto the truck prompted a mass mobilization of passers-by.
(Right): Similar stills in place at the famous Le Brun distillery

The fire should be lit with vine wood. Not only does this guarantee that no chemicals enter the production process and ensure that none of the raw materials goes to waste, it also creates a sense of ritual that is essential to the perpetuity of any national tradition

The arak production process begins with the grapes. For our purposes they should be white Lebanese grapes, preferably Obeideh (although Ugni Blanc, the grape of choice in the Cognac region of France, can also be used). The Obeideh should be crushed slowly and allowed to ferment naturally without the use of yeast

Baladi

Elias Najeeb Karam, is known in Zabougha as Abou Shanab (literally father of the moustache), because of his magnificent whiskers. Every year, like many of his contemporaries in the village, he makes homemade arak, called *baladi*, from his still.

'Nearly everyone has a still in the area,' he explains. At seventy-five, there is little you can't tell him about arak-making and the much debated benefits of *baladi* over the commercial brands.

October and November are traditionally the months when arak *baladi* is made. The law technically prohibits the home distiller from owning a still without a permit, but in the absence of a clampdown, which would be unprecedented, the household *kerki* (still) will bubble away as it has done for generations.

The process is relatively simple. If you have a still, several big plastic barrels and a densitometer to test for alcoholic content, then all you need is a lot of grapes, aniseed and water.

Crushing the grapes the traditional way

The aniseed is added during the second distillation and once again in the final stage, when 2 kilos are added to every 20 litres. For Abou Shanab, the whole process takes three days. He makes 100 litres each season. For this he needs 400 kilos of grapes for which he pays around LL200,000 and 20 kilos of aniseed at LL100,000. The 60 litres of bottled water cost LL50,000 and a ton of firewood for his still costs LL300,000.

Factoring in his time and effort, he believes that it costs him LL825,000 to make his 100 litres, which boils down to just over LL8,000 per litre. The market rate for *baladi mtalat* (arak that is thrice distilled) is LL12,000, but Abou Shanab is at pains to point out that he never sells what he makes. 'That would be illegal,' he says with just the slightest of twinkles in his eye.

But why does he do it? Why doesn't he just go to the shops and buy it off the shelves? 'You don't know what is put in the other stuff,' he warns, no doubt referring to the commercial brands. 'I want to know what I'm drinking.'

Georges Haibeh takes a break after tending to his still

Abou Shanab enjoys a tipple

This page and following page:
Picking the grapes is a family
affair

Arak Makers

Arak Le Brun

Domaine des Tourelles, producer of arguably Lebanon's greatest arak, is a winery and distillery steeped in a tradition that blends the Bekaa's wine- and arak-making culture with Lebanon's strong Francophone ties. Established in 1868 by a French adventurer, François-Eugène Brun, Domaine des Tourelles played an important role in the early years of the Lebanon's modern wine industry. Seventy years later, François-Eugène's grandson, *the* Pierre Brun, inherited the winery at a time when Lebanon was enduring the birth pangs of independence. He steered the company through its most successful period and stood shoulder to shoulder with the people of his adopted country during the darkest days of the civil war. Although the company is still thriving, when Pierre Brun died in 2000, a Franco-Lebanese dynasty came to an end. Nonetheless, today, Pierre Brun's legendary arak is still ranked amongst Lebanon's finest.

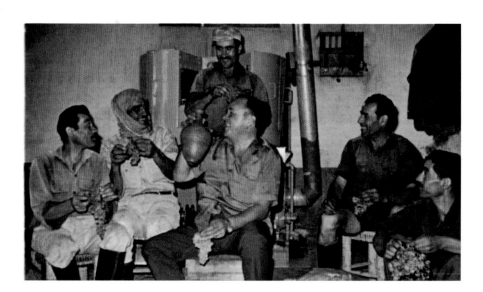

Pierre Brun enjoys a happy moment with his staff

Le Brun, arguably the most
famous Lebanese arak

The story begins in 1860, when François-Eugène, then a twenty-four-year-old French military engineer from Chezery Forens in the Rhône Alps, arrived in Lebanon to work on the Beirut–Damascus road after he and a friend had been recruited in Marseilles. On arriving in the Bekaa, he immediately fell in love with the rural town of Chtaura, then part of Syria.

Months later, his boss, Herr Ziller, the project's chief engineer, was murdered in his sleep by thieves looking for the payroll he had picked up the day before from the Turkish authorities in Beirut. As Frau Ziller made plans to return to her children in Switzerland, François-Eugène stepped in to buy their house, and in doing so, put down the first roots of what would be Domaine des Tourelles.

At that time and in that place a house needed a woman. Brun wooed and won Valerie Brunache, the daughter of a French hotel owner from Chtaura. They had five children, three boys and two girls, and before he died in 1896 he had founded Lebanon's first genuinely commercial winery, the wines from which had already won a medal at the London wine fair. The winery was inherited by his sons, Louis and Paul. There was another voyage to London and another *médaille*. Louis Brun married Aline Faure, another French expatriate, with whom he had two children, André and Pierre, who was born in 1920.

Success, however, was touched with tragedy. In November 1936, Asian flu swept the region, taking with it Louis Brun and his sister, who was living as a nun in Jerusalem, and two of their nephews. Pierre Brun, then aged sixteen, would never come to terms with the loss of his father, and his sense of personal tragedy was to be compounded over twenty years later by the death of his brother, André, a French army officer and veteran of the fighting in Indo-China, who died in Algeria.

Those who knew Pierre Brun remember him as a bon viveur, who loved his food. 'He would travel for good food,' says Nayla Issa-el Khoury, the distillery's new co-owner. 'But he was a very secretive man. Everything he made in his life was a secret. Fortunately, we still employ the same staff, so we know how to make his arak,' she adds laughing.

But his workers loved him for it. Many stayed on at the winery after

Facing page: Elie Issa oversees the sorting of the grapes

working hours to look after the premises, especially during the war, a period during which Brun chose not to flee to the safety of France. Today, still situated on the main Damascus road, Domaine des Tourelles winery is a haven of tranquillity on this now busy thoroughfare. The estate is full of elegant reminders of a bygone era: honey-bees settle round the garden pond; a distressed motorbike lies near the beehive and an old pair of black loafers lie among the clutter of a potting shed amid the debris of another life in another time. The chaos of Chtaura, the bustling border town, is suddenly a million miles away.

Across the field lies the distillery and winery, with its elegant blue door that announces the legend of Tourelles. The buildings, although very much functioning concerns, are also a museum to Lebanon's pre-war wine and arak culture and its relationship with the community. Above the sacks of Hina aniseed, destined for the arak, hang faded photos of Brun's ancestors and groups of workers alongside framed confirmation certificates of workers' children. A pith helmet here, a pair of working boots there are all reminders of a rural tradition that is sadly on the wane.

In the main house, Brun's bedroom is as it was when he died: suit trousers hang on a rack; a dusty record collection sits in a cardboard box. Inside a wardrobe is a plastic Christmas tree wrapped in cellophane. 'Pierre Brun hated Christmas,' explains Elie Issa, Issa-Koury's partner. 'It reminded him of the death of family members.' He looks at a faded photo of André Brun next to a framed row of medals. 'He never went out at Christmas. We would always have to visit him.'

Domaine des Tourelles's output until the mid-70s had been roughly 80 per cent wine and 20 per cent arak. The outbreak of the Lebanese civil war changed all that, as a combination of Brun's age and the unpredictable security situation made wine-making too precarious. Brun realized that wine-making required more effort and, given that there was no broad-based domestic market as there is today, a decision was taken to concentrate on arak. Brun may not have known it at the time, but the decision was to lead to the birth of something special. Even other arak producers will grudgingly

Facing page: The gateway to the Le Brun distillery and winery in Chtaura

concede that old man Brun's tipple has become a touchstone. What's the secret? Issa gives nothing away. 'We make our arak in the traditional *artisana*, using only the best aniseed.' Pierre Brun may have had French blood, but Lebanon was his home. He is buried in the family tomb in Jdeita, next to his Lebanese wife, who died one year before him.

Arak Massaya

If Le Brun is the king of Lebanese commercial arak, Massaya is the heir apparent. Founded in 1997 by Sami and Ramzi Ghosn, two brothers who believed in Lebanon and its traditions, Massaya is both a distillery and winery. While the brothers' wines may have won laurels and plaudits from the world's finest critics and sommeliers, in Lebanon the Ghosns are, albeit grudgingly, credited with dragging arak – a drink that until the mid-90s was seen as an unfashionable throwback – kicking and screaming into the world of boutique goods with their own brand in the famous blue bottles. The launch of Massaya arak dovetailed nicely with the first genuine stirrings

Arak-making at Massaya is set within a rural tradition and the notion of eating in good company with arak

of post-war optimism in Lebanon since it represented summer dining and carefree, beautiful people.

The brothers, who had been brought up on organic foods and felt that there might be a market for traditional rural produce, first ventured into making *dibs* (molasses) and *kishik* (Lebanese porridge); but it was the arak that flew.

'In 1993, we rented a distillery to make the arak, which we sold from our parents' pharmacy at $50 the gallon,' remembers Sami Ghosn. 'When people started coming back for more, I sensed we might be on to something and sourced some clay jars from an old factory in Beit Shabeb. Each jar cost me one *lira dahab* (gold coin).' And so it began. The brothers had the product; now all they had to do was sell it. They decided to move away from the traditional white and green bottles. They wanted something different and which would reflect Lebanon. They went for blue. 'Blue in Arabic is *fairuz* and also the name of Lebanon's most beloved female singer,' explains Ramzi. 'It is also the sky and sea. To us it was Lebanon.' The brainstorming paid off. The arak, now out of the bulk glass flagons and wearing the blue livery decorated with instinctive Arabic calligraphy, hit the market like a tsunami.

'No one could have predicted the impact,' says Sami. 'At the time, arak was dead and whisky was king. We came along with our blue bottles and at

The poplars at Massaya with the Anti-Lebanon mountains behind them

first they said "Pah! They're selling glass," but then they tasted it. I am telling you, we started a revolution. Maybe it is arrogant to say this, but the others were doing such a bad job with the arak that we felt we could do better. Today, Arak Massaya can be found on every continent except Australia.'

Not bad for a revolution.

Arak Touma

The Toumas of the Bekaa have been in the alcohol business for over a century, producing arak since 1888. Today, the family arak business has expanded into wine and two branches of the Touma family have wineries: Clos St Thomas, owned by Sayeed Touma, and Heritage, owned by his nephew, Dargham. Strictly speaking, the Touma family has been making wine since 1958, with the Cinsault grapes used for arak, but it was only with the end of the civil war in 1990 that Sayeed and Dargham set about realizing their dream of making quality wine for an international market.

A young Sayeed Touma in a lighthearted mood with glass of restorative arak

But it is arak in which the family's tradition is steeped. In 1888, the Touma distillery was founded by Gebran Touma, Sayeed's grandfather. Gebran was one of those canny, hard-working Lebanese who took no chances in ensuring the future of the business he had established. Before he died he left instructions that his family bury him in the vineyard.

'He knew that if we did that no one would sell up the land,' explains Sayeed. 'He knew that they would not want anyone saying their kids had sold out and had literally sold their father.' Gebran's son, Tanios, was sent to Brazil during the First World War to escape conscription into the Ottoman army. 'He was only nine, but when he was born my grandfather registered him as older than he was,' says Sayeed. 'It was the thing to do back then. It was thought that older people were taken more seriously, so sometimes a father would give the son a head start.'

The Brazil trip was not a happy experience for the young Tanios, who found work on a ranch with other Lebanese. One night, protecting his cattle from rustlers, a shoot-out erupted during which he killed seven cattle thieves. Self-defence or not, he was forced to return to a changed Lebanon. The Turks had gone and the French were running the show, and there was nothing to do but work with his brothers in the family business. In 1946, the brothers parted corporate company, leaving Tanios the sole owner of Touma Arak. However, in 1948, on his way back from a trip to Palestine, he was killed in a car accident on the Damascus road. His son, Rachid, along with his mother Adelle and brothers Elias, Sayeed and Fadlo went on to found Société Rachid Tanios Touma & Frères and build the Arak Touma brand. Today, Elias, Sayeed and Fadlo are joined by Rachid's children, Tanios, Walid, Jihad and Nadine in keeping alive a proud tradition.

The Touma family is from Qab Elias, the first town on the road from Chtaura into the western Bekaa. The family is acutely aware of the proud tradition they are upholding. Driving north to Chtaura, Dargham points to the slopes of the Lebanon mountain range. 'See that?' he says, indicating a huge frieze on the side of the hill. 'It's the sun temple. The Romans built it. It's supposed to be one of the points where the sun first hits the Bekaa when

Facing page: Arak Touma

it rises. We have an ancient tradition here on the Bekaa. We supplied Rome with grapes and wheat.'

Back at Clos St Thomas winery, Sayeed Touma brings out a bottle of arak and pours half into a sizeable tumbler. He then pours in the water, allowing it to overflow until he is satisfied with the ratio. Then with a flourish he takes a sip and hands me the glass. 'This is what I really know,' he whispers, as if admitting to preferring arak is somehow a bit uncool. 'And I learned it all by these,' he says, putting a finger to his nose and then to his mouth.

Ghantous Abu Raad

Look on the shelves of the best Lebanese supermarkets and you will find the colourful and elegant bottles of Domaine Wardy, one of Lebanon's new generation of wine producers. The bottles testify to the New World wine revolution in which single varietal wines – Cabernet Sauvignon, Chardonnay, Merlot, Syrah and so on – have entered the consciousness of the modern wine drinker. Selim Wardy, owner of Domaine Wardy, knows this is the way forward and is committed to harnessing his wines on the back of today's wine culture.

But the story of Domaine Wardy must be traced back to 1893, when two of Zahleh's major arak-making families, the Ghantous and the Abu Raad, joined forces to produce one of Lebanon's oldest and most famous araks. At the time, wine was for church and Lebanon was by and large an arak-drinking nation, despite the Islamic strictures of its Ottoman masters, who it is generally agreed, turned a blind eye. The term 'industry' must be used lightly. This was a rural community; the unregulated distillation process was often fraught with danger and there were many accidents in which more than a few home distillers lost their lives either by poisoning or blowing themselves up using unstable stills. It was an occupational hazard that carried on well into the twentieth century. 'Not that long ago, we had some scares,' recalls Selim Wardy, who remembers hearing of an accident at the old Ghantous, Abou Raad factory, when a member of staff recklessly threw away a lit cigarette butt, nearly wiping out the entire workforce. 'He was lucky not be killed. But, what a way to die,' he laughs. 'As it was, he lived to be ninety.'

Facing page: Ghantous & Abou Raad, an old and popular Lebanese brand

The Wardy family's involvement with arak began in 1971, when Selim's father bought a controlling interest in Ghantous, Abou Raad arak, when it ran into financial difficulties. The investment allowed for modernization of the plant, and, by 1974, the brand had become Lebanon's leading popular arak. In 1996, the Wardys bought out the remaining shareholders of Ghantous, Abou Raad and went it alone. With a free rein at the arak factory they began to give full expression to their wine and arak ambitions, immediately launching the premium Arak Wardy, an inheritor of a proud tradition.

Arak as-Samir

Selim Nakad, who with his three brothers owns the Nakad winery and distillery, insists, like a good Bekaa man, that arak is in his blood. Outside his house and winery he has what he claims is a Bronze Age wine press, unearthed in his garden. Surely here was proof that the Nakads and the people of Jdeita are the heirs of a millennia-old tradition. 'The product of the grape has always been with us,' he says. 'The church always made wine,

The Nakad family have a strong and proud history in arak- and wine-making

Faving page: The arak still at the Nakad winery in Jdeita

even before the nineteenth century, and we always made arak and smuggled it over the mountains on mules, hidden in barrels disguised with honey on top – not that the Turks really minded.' Selim's father was originally a shoemaker who also made arak and small quantities of wine on the side in a village that boasted around twenty-five stills at the turn of the century. 'It was a self-sufficient community. The people would spend summer and autumn making their *mounie* (winter supplies) and then it was a case of hibernation for winter. People would eat, drink and sleep. That's why we had eight children in our family!'

Arak Kfifane

General Bitar proudly shows off his arak

Retired General Joseph Bitar is not one to give up easily. Bitar, whose ancestors have been living in the hills of Kfifane since 1770, can look back on

a life of action and a degree of sporting excellence. As a career soldier from 1943 until 1977, he was present at all the Lebanese army's 'major' engagements before the outbreak of the civil war and was the army equestrian champion in the early 60s. Retirement proved no more peaceful. He took up fishing, only to be machine-gunned while angling in his boat off the coast of Batroun. The bullets failed to write off the old warrior though, and in 1991 he went on to make what he considers 'probably the best arak in the world'.

The general explains that his arak is sold successfully by word of mouth. 'I

Labelling is done by hand

only make 1,800 litres a year and my margins are very small,' he barks. 'Still, I have my customers and they know what they like.'

Surely his boast is a trifle exaggerated? He gives a steely stare that is no doubt known to many an ex-soldier. 'Taste it and then tell me,' he says, dropping two enormous ice cubes into a small arak glass. It is only 10.00 AM and the sun, although still revving its engine, is beginning to make its presence felt. The hue of Bitar's arak is deep white, almost marble-like. The taste is incredibly clean despite the 65 per cent strength. Satisfied, the general leans back in his seat. 'This region is one of olives, grapes and figs. This is our land. We need to get the most out of it.'

Arak Musar

The late Auberon Waugh, one of the most respected British wine writers of the last fifty years, called Château Musar one of the 'great wines of the world'.

This page and facing page: Musar, one of the most famous names in the world of wine, also makes a premium arak

But being Lebanese, it also makes a fine arak. The winery was founded in 1930 by Gaston Hochar, father of the current owners, Serge and Ronald Hochar, who wanted to upgrade the image of wine-making in Lebanon. Forty-nine years after it was established, Musar struck gold, making the headlines in the British press after receiving rave reviews at the Bristol wine fair. It has not looked back since and its reputation was enhanced further when Serge Hochar was voted *Decanter's* Man of the Year in 1984 for his commitment to producing wine during the Lebanese civil war. Hochar is a firm believer in the quality and magic of the Lebanese *terroir* and the fruits it produces. 'Throughout history the wines of Lebanon have been known to the world, and when I discovered the quality of the fruits of Lebanon I knew that this was no accident. If it were not for this, I would have done something else, something that would have lacked the passion of wine. I was profoundly inspired by the power of life in this country, which goes beyond our understanding, and I thought it would be a very good idea to show that what we can produce from these grapes can be something fascinating, something to express this life of Lebanon, the Lebanon of the way we live our daily lives. The way we vibrate is exceptional. Why? I don't know. It is present in the fruits, the vegetables and the people.'

Ksarak

Château Ksara is the best-selling wine in the Middle East. It is also Lebanon's biggest and oldest winery, producing two million bottles annually. It began

The bottling plant at Château Ksara

life in 1857, when Jesuit brothers inherited and began farming a 25-hectare plot of land to produce Lebanon's first non-sweet red wine. In doing so, they laid the foundations of Lebanon's modern wine industry.

At the end of the First World War, France was mandated to govern Lebanon. Its military and administrative machine moved in, bringing with it thousands of French soldiers and civil servants, for whom wine was an integral part of their culture. Ksara was in a position to supply Lebanon's new administrators, and by the time the French left in 1946 Lebanon had embraced the Francophone experience with a passion that can still be felt today. During the next thirty years, Ksara maintained its position as Lebanon's most popular wine, while Lebanon grew into a cosmopolitan and convivial hub, where Western tastes were eagerly adopted.

In 1972, the Vatican encouraged its monasteries and missions around the world to sell off any commercial activities. By then, Ksara was a profitable entity, producing over one million bottles annually and representing 85 per cent of Lebanese production. When the order to sell came through, the winery was optioned to a consortium of Lebanese businessmen, and in August 1973 was sold for $3.2 million. It was during this time that the winery launched its own

The sophisticated and modern French still at Château Ksara

arak brand, Ksarak, the brainchild of the first managing director, Jean-Pierre Sara. Today it is among Lebanon's most popular and best-selling premium araks. Ksarak is, like the *eau de vie* of Cognac, made from Ugni Blanc, one of the earliest imported white grapes in Lebanon, and aged for two years in clay. Château Ksara also makes an *eau de vie* that rivals the best cognacs.

Arak Fakra

Carlos Adem's great-uncle, Sheikh Nabih El Khazen, began making arak in 1919, producing what was arguably Lebanon's first branded and labelled arak. After his death in 1931, the business declined, but Adem, who has vineyards in France and Argentina as well as Lebanon, revived the tradition in 1985. Within three years it had achieved a 50 per cent market share and is today still one of the most popular and visible araks in the country.

Top: An early label from one of Lebanon's oldest producers

Bottom: Fakra's new ageing room

Arak Kefraya

Founded in 1978, Kefraya, whose majority shareholder is the Charismatic Druze politician Walid Jumblatt – understood to be a devotee of arak – is Lebanon's second biggest wine producer and the vineyard that gave the world Comte de M '96, one of Lebanon's most exciting Lebanese wines of the post-war era. Château Kefraya's grapes are grown in the 300-hectare Kefraya estate and are subject to an internal quality control similar to an *appellation d'origine controllé*. The arak is one of the most respected on the Lebanese market.

Collecting grapes

Overleaf: Château Kefraya's owner Michel de Bustros inspects the harvest with his foreman

Mezze

Mezze is the selection of small dishes – hummus, aubergine, stuffed vineleaves, yoghurt, tabbouleh and the like – with which many of you will be familiar if you have dined at Lebanese, Turkish and Greek restaurants. Mezze can be eaten either alone or as appetizers for the main meat event – in Lebanon normally grilled beef, lamb, chicken or *koftah* kebabs, grilled or fried fish.

But what to drink with mezze? Most people get it wrong. It doesn't mean they won't enjoy their mezze. It just means they probably aren't getting the most out of it.

Strictly speaking, wine doesn't work with Lebanese mezze – or any other Mediterranean mezze for that matter. Tabbouleh, the popular salad made with parsley, tomato, mint, lemon and onions, is stuffed with acidity. Who needs to pile it on more with a white or rosé wine? This is where arak, or any of the other Mediterranean, aniseed-flavoured, grape-based spirits for that matter, is the perfect match. With tabbouleh, it will not be overwhelmed by lemon; on the contrary, its alkaline properties will neutralize the acidity while the aniseed will aid digestion.

Arak gives balance to the mezze experience, which involves a frantic, if enjoyable, journey hopping from dish to dish and flavour to flavour. When you are eating a range of foods such as *fatoush* (salad), *makanek* (sausages), *fatayer* (cheese pastry) or *Fassoulia* (beans), it is very difficult to match them all with wine. Arak's body means it will carry all the tastes from one dish to another by rinsing the palate, refreshing the taste buds – an important process that allows the diner to get the best out of the mezze's spectrum of flavours.

Although many of the following dishes have peasant origins, the pairings have been thoughtfully considered over the generations. *Awarma* (chopped meat preserved in fat) should technically be suited to wine because it is salty and heavy in fat, but when it is mixed with eggs – notoriously difficult to pair with wine – to make the hearty mountain breakfast of *bayd awarma*, it is arak that comes to the rescue, and that is why the people of the mountain drink it with

Facing page: Elias Fadel pouring arak in his famous and eponymous restaurant

breakfast. Likewise, raw *kibbeh* (puréed meat) or raw liver are washed down with arak. For raw *kibbeh*, a dish that must be served with mint, onions (especially in the morning) and tabbouleh, arak is needed to cope with the mint, a nightmare to pair with wine (if you eat a mint leaf and then take a sip of any wine, there will be an aftertaste suggesting that the wine is not fit for drinking).

Arak is the summer drink with summer food. One must remember that in Lebanon, even until very recently there was summer and winter food. There was little refrigeration in the mountains, so all winter food – preserves or *mouni* – had to be prepared in the summer and autumn.

So wine in winter, arak in summer. It's a clever and hugely practical cycle. In September the Lebanese mountain farmer picks his grapes. Traditionally, he and his family would eat as many as they could before crushing them and fermenting them to make wine. From October to February he is faced with a dead season. All winter he would stay at home, eat his *mouni* – lentils, hummos, *bourghol* (crushed bulgur wheat), *awarma*, spiced *labneh* balls, all of which go well with wine incidentally – cook around the *sobia* (the traditional mountain stove) and make sure that his wife would bear another child the following summer.

He would also drink wine, which would have been made in late autumn. It would be fresh and tasty, but in the absence of oak barrels it had to be stored in clay jars, which are not the most efficient storage vessels; the wines are good only until March when, because of oxidation, they will start to turn into vinegar. The farmer knows this by taste and will immediately take his ageing wine and triple distill it either on his own still or by renting his landlord's. He has his arak, a stable neutral product that will keep until summer.

The arak mountain tradition came out of a storage issue. The problem with wine is not the production; anyone who knows grapes can make wine. The historical problem of wine was storing it. The Lebanese farmer solved this problem by drinking it young, and that's why the Lebanese like the Cinsault grape because it is a variety that allows you to make wine that can be consumed quickly and, when it starts to show high volatile acidity, be transformed into arak.

Facing page: The arak and mezze experience as demonstrated by Marie-Ange "Kiki" Bokassa, the half-Lebanese daughter of former African leader Jean-Bedel Bokassa

Arak Breakfast

Raw Liver with Mint and Onion
Sawada nayeh maa naana ou bassal

1 whole lamb's liver
100 g / 3 ½ oz lamb fat
10 spring onions
A few sprigs of mint
Salt and pepper to taste

Chop the liver and the fat into small squares and serve on a dish garnished with fresh mint. On a side-plate serve whole fresh green onions together with some salt and pepper on the side. Recommended for those who enjoy a hearty breakfast or who have worked up an appetite perhaps from a long, pre-breakfast walk. Traditionally, this dish is eaten on a Sunday morning, when one can enjoy it without rushing to work, especially if, as recommended, it is washed down with arak.

Raw Kaftah

Kaftah nayeh

600 g / 1 lb 4 oz chopped leg of mutton
2 medium onions
1 sprig of parsley
Salt and pepper to taste
Mint to garnish
Olive oil

Knead the finely minced meat until it becomes dough-like. Finely chop the onions and parsley. Season with salt and pepper and knead well together. Pour on olive oil and garnish with mint. For those to whom raw meat is still a step into the unknown, the *kaftah* can also be spread on pitta bread and grilled in the oven until crisp, or it can be put on skewers and placed on the barbeque.

Meat and Eggs
Bayd be awarma

1 kg / 2 lb lamb chopped into small pieces
1 kg / 2 lb lamb fat chopped into small pieces
Spices: 10 cardamom pods, 10 bay leaves, 2 tsp allspice, 2 tsp salt
6 eggs

First prepare the *awarma*: Heat the fat until it starts to melt, then lower the heat and remove any gristle. Add the chopped meat and spices and cook on a low heat for 60 minutes, stirring from time to time until the meat is soft and cooked. Leave to cool before pouring into airtight jars, to be used as needed.

Heat the *awarma* until the fat has melted and the mixture is warm. Break the eggs on top and cook for 5 minutes.

A great way to start the day! Don't be put off by the high fat content. This is a sensational cooked breakfast, one whose origins can be traced to the mountains of Lebanon, where calorie-burning, outdoor-living farmers had no such worries about cholesterol. In the old days awarma used to be cooked in large quantities over wooden fires where the whole family and even neighbours would gather to help in its preparation. It was considered part of the *mouneh* or winter supplies that were prepared in the summer.

Cold Vegetarian Dishes

An Aubergine Dip
Baba ghannouj

2 large round aubergines
2 medium tomatoes, chopped
1 small onion, chopped
Juice of a squeezed lemon
Olive oil, salt and pepper to taste

Bake two round aubergines, turning them as the sides burn (roughly every 5 minutes). When the skin is evenly burned place the aubergines in a bowl. When cooled, peel off the skin under running water and wash the pulp. Leave in a strainer until dry, then cut into squares. Chop the onion and tomatoes into small squares. Mix together the aubergine pulp, onions, tomatoes, lemon juice and olive oil and add a pinch of salt and pepper. Serve as a dip.

Aubergine Purée
Mtabal

1 large round aubergine
4 to 5 tbs tahini
Juice of a squeezed lemon
1 clove of garlic
Olive oil and a pinch of salt to taste
A handful of chopped parsley and sour pomegranate seeds

Bake two round aubergines, turning them every five minutes until the sides are burned. When the skin is evenly burned place the aubergines in a bowl. When cooled, peel off the skin under running water and wash the pulp. Finely chop the garlic, season with salt and put the mixture into a blender until you have a smooth, thick liquid. Add the tahini then lemon juice to taste, and mix thoroughly. Serve on platters or individual small plates and garnish with parsley and pomegranate seeds.

A Bean Dish
Fassoulia matabaleh

200 g / 7 oz / 2 cups fresh fava beans
Juice of a squeezed lemon
1 clove of garlic
Salt and olive oil to taste

Place the *fassoulia* (fava beans) in a pan of water and bring to the boil. Reduce the heat and simmer for 90 minutes (for dry beans) or 45 minutes (for fresh beans), or until soft. Add the lemon juice, the crushed clove of garlic, a pinch of salt and some olive oil and mix together. Serve as a side dish or appetizer.

Chickpea Dip

Hummus

200 g / 7 oz / 2 cups dry chickpeas
4 to 5 tbsp tahini
Juice of a squeezed lemon
2 cloves of garlic, coarsely crushed
A few sprigs of mint
Olive oil and salt to taste

Cover the chickpeas in water and soak overnight with a teaspoon of bicarbonate of soda. The next day, rinse the chickpeas thoroughly, add fresh water and bring to the boil. Reduce the heat and simmer for two hours or until the chickpeas are soft. Drain the chickpeas and pour into a blender with two crushed cloves of garlic, the tahini and salt to taste. When the mixture becomes creamy, add the lemon juice and water to obtain the desired consistency. Serve in small dishes with olive oil poured on top; garnish with mint.

Spicy Goat Cheese Dip
Shankleesh

1 ready-made 'ball' of *shankleesh*
1 small onion
1 large tomato
Olive oil and salt to taste

Shankleesh is prepared from *laban* (skimmed yoghurt). The laban is boiled and stirred until the mixture separates into liquid and solid. The solid part is the arisheh acid, which is strained through a cheesecloth. Once all the liquid is drained off, special herbs such as soft pepper and cumin are added to the mixture, which is then rolled and kneaded into small balls and left in the sun to dry. The dried balls are then placed in glass jars covered with a linen fabric to allow the *shankleesh* to mature, a process that takes three weeks. All the while, the balls are regularly checked for mould, which is wiped off. When they are mature, the balls are plunged for minute in an olive oil and lemon 'bath' before being coated with *zaatar* (dried thyme). For those who want a shortcut to *shankleesh* heaven ready-made balls can be purchased.

Chop the *shankleesh*, onion and tomato into small squares, add oil, a pinch of salt, a sprinkle of red paprika and mix together. Serve as a dip.

Tomatoes with Sumac

Banadoura maa sumeq

2 beef tomatoes

1 tbs sumac

1 tbs mayonnaise

1 whole head of garlic

Olive oil and salt to taste

Mint to garnish

In Lebanon, beef tomatoes are called *banadoura jabalieh* or mountain tomatoes, which are planted in the mountains and have a distinct taste. They are very popular even when green. The fruit of the sumac tree is frequently used in Lebanese cooking.

To prepare the garlic purée, crush all the garlic cloves, add a tablespoon of mayonnaise and a tablespoon of olive oil and blend.

Slice the tomatoes, spread them with the garlic mix and sprinkle with sumac, olive oil and salt. Garnish with mint.

Blended Herbs
Tahweesheh

Tahweesheh is a mixture of basil, parsley, marjoram, onion, orange peel, cumin, black pepper, salt, *mardakoush* and mint blended together with rose petals and added to *burghul* (crushed wheat). It is used in many *kibbeh* dishes, both meat and vegetarian.

Potatoes with Burghul
Kibbeh batata

4 large potatoes
100 g / 3½ oz / 1 cup of *burghul*
1 large onion

A handful of *mardakoush* (marjoram), *zaatar* (thyme), coriander, and mint,
1 teaspoon of cloves and cumin powder (an alternative for *tahweesheh*)
   Olive oil, salt and pepper to taste

Soak the burghul in cold water for 10 minutes. Drain and squeeze out the excess water. Set aside. Peel the potatoes and boil in lightly salted water. When they are cooked, drain them and mash into a purée with a fork (the purée does not have to be very smooth). Chop the onion in a mixer and add either tahweesheh or the herbs, together with the burghul, salt and pepper. Mix with the mashed potatoes and serve with a sprinkling of olive oil.

This and the following dish are favourites among vegetarians. Traditionally they were eaten either by those who were fasting and wanted a light meal to break the fast or those who simply could not afford meat.

Tomato Kibbeh
Kibbeh banadoura

5 large ripe tomatoes
100 g / 3 ½ oz / 1 cup *burghul*
1 large onion

A handful of *mardakoush*, *zaatar*, coriander, and mint, 1 teaspoon of cloves
and cumin powder (an alternative for *tahweesheh*)
    Olive oil, salt and pepper to taste

Soak the *burghul* in cold water for 10 minutes. Drain and squeeze out the
excess water. Set aside. Chop the tomatoes and onion into small pieces and
add to the *tahweesheh* or the herbs, with the freshly soaked *burghul*. Add
olive oil, salt and pepper to taste and serve.

Meat Dishes

Fine Raw Lamb
Lahmeh Melsi

This dish a specialty from South Lebanon, where women would grind the meat on a *blatah* (a stone).

> 200 g / 7 oz fresh lamb
> 100 g / 3 ½ oz *tahweesheh*
> A few sprigs of mint leaves
> Olive oil, salt and pepper to taste
> Green onions and radishes (optional)

Put the lamb in a blender and mince until very fine and pink, then cool in the refrigerator for at least 2 hours. Season with salt and pepper and serve on a plate with the tahweesheh to one side, and garnish with mint and olive oil. To bring out the taste, eat with green onions and radishes.

Raw Mince Purée
Kibbeh nayeh

250 g / 8 oz / 2 ½ cups fine *burghul*
1 kg / 2 lb lean lamb or beef
1 large onion
1 tsp white pepper
3 tsp cinnamon powder
A few sprigs of mint leaves
Salt, pepper and olive oil to taste

Soak the *burghul* in cold water for 10 minutes. Drain and squeeze out the excess water. Set aside. Crush the onion until it becomes watery. Use a food processor (or *blatah*) to finely grind the meat. Transfer the meat to a large mixing bowl and add the *burghul*, the onion, white pepper, cinnamon and seasoning. Knead the mixture well, adding, every now and then, a dash of cold water. (Those who don't have the energy to knead can process small portions at a time using a food processor, but traditionally *kibbeh* was kneaded with the palm of the hand, and the fingers kept dipping in cold water.) Place on a serving platter and chill well in the refrigerator. Remove just before serving and garnish with olive oil and mint.

Fried Kibbeh

Kibbeh miq'lieh

500 g / 1 lb flank of beef

200 g / 7 oz / 2 cups *burghul*

1 large onion

1 tsp salt and pepper to taste

3 tsp cinnamon powder

For the stuffing

100 g / 3 ½ oz finely chopped meat

1 large onion

50 g / 2 oz / ½ cup pine kernels

2 tbs oil

Prepare the *kibbeh* as for *kibbeh nayeh* (page 122). Then prepare the stuffing by browning the ingredients separately in oil and then mixing them. Make a ball of *kibbeh* the size of an egg. Dig in with the finger while holding the ball in the hollow of the other hand. When the walls are no thicker than half a centimetre, fill with stuffing and pinch closed. (Fry the *kibbeh* balls in oil, or bake them in the oven at a medium heat for 40 minutes.) They can be served warm or cold.

Grilled *Kafta*

Kafta mishweh

600 g / 1 lb 3 ½ oz minced lamb or beef
2 medium onions
1 sprig of parsley
Salt and pepper to taste

Knead the meat finely until it becomes dough-like. Then chop the onions and parsley equally finely. Add salt and pepper and knead well together. *Kafta* can be served raw with a sprinkle of olive oil or grilled on skewers over a barbeque or under an oven grill. It can also be served on a slice of pitta bread with roughly chopped parsley and onion slices with a sprinkle of sumac.

Chickpea Dip with Beef

Hummus ma lahmeh

200 g / 7 oz minced beef

200 g / 7 oz / 2 cups dry chickpeas

4 to 5 tbs tahini

Juice of a squeezed lemon

2 cloves of garlic

100 g / 3 ½ oz / 1 cup of pine kernels

Salt and pepper to taste

Prepare the hummus (page 111). Fry the meat and the pine kernels in olive oil, and season with salt and pepper. Place the meat mixture on top of the hummus and serve.

Grilled Vegetables

Batenjen (aubergine)
Kousa (squash)
Fliefleh (green peppers)
Qarnabeet (cauliflower)

These vegetables are all traditionally used in mezze dishes. In the mountain communities they are homegrown and are dietary staples. They are also used in stews, stuffed with rice and/or meat.

Dice all the vegetables and grill. Garnish with a handful of sesame seeds.

Salads

Thyme
Zaatar

Zaatar (thyme) can come in different varieties but the leafy varieties are particularly good for salads. After washing the leaves well, cut an onion into small squares and squeeze a lemon and mix with a pinch of salt and some olive oil. *Zaatar barry* (wild thyme) is especially delicious, with a sharp taste that goes well with arak.

Tomato Salad
Banadoura

4 regular tomatoes
3 sprigs of mint / 1 tsp dried mint
Juice of a squeezed lemon
Salt and olive oil to taste

Dice the tomatoes into squares, add some cut mint leaves (or dried mint when not in season), some freshly squeezed lemon juice, salt and olive oil.

Purslane

Baqli

Pick the leaves from the stalks and wash thoroughly. Cut the onion into thin round slices, add sumac, salt and olive oil.

Tabbouleh

2 bunches parsley
3 large tomatoes
A handful of mint leaves
1 small onion
Juice of 1–2 lemons
25 g / ¾ oz / ¼ cup *burghul*
Salt, pepper and olive oil to taste

Wash the parsley, mint and tomatoes. Finely chop the parsley and the mint and put aside. Dice the tomatoes into small squares and place on top of the chopped parsley. Finely chop the onion, season and mix well. Prepare the *burghul* by soaking it in cold water for 10 minutes. Drain and squeeze out the excess water. Pour the lemon juice over the *burghul* to soften it, then mix all the ingredients together, adding the olive oil.

Lebanese Salad with Crispy Bread
Fatoush

½ head of lettuce

3 large tomatoes

1 bunch parsley

A handful of mint and *baqli* (purslane) leaves

6 small radishes

4 green onions

1 medium green pepper

Coriander (optional)

Juice of a squeezed lemon

1 tsp sumac

Salt, pepper and olive oil to taste

1 whole medium pitta bread toasted or fried and broken into small squares

Finely cut the lettuce leaves, the parsley and the mint (and coriander if you are a fan), and dice the tomatoes and the radishes into small squares (but not as small as for *tabouleh*). Cut the onion and pepper into small circles, add the *baqli* and the lemon juice. Season with salt and pepper and the sumac and mix well. Add the bread just before serving, so that it stays crunchy.

Nibbles to Accompany Arak

Pickles, olives, pistachio nuts, carrots, cucumbers, pickled garlic, sun dried tomatoes.

With pitta bread garnished with mint or basil: *Jibneh baladi* (country cheese), *Labneh maazeh* (goat's yoghurt).

Arak Sorbet

200 g /7 oz / 2 cups water

100 g / 3 ½ oz / 1 cup sugar

Rind of 1 lemon

Juice of 2 squeezed lemons

100 g / 3 ½ oz / 1 cup arak

Boil the water, sugar and lemon rind for 7 minutes. Add the lemon juice and strain the mixture. Cool the sugar 'syrup' and season with arak, before freezing lightly. Take one egg white and beat it lightly, before stirring into the partially frozen sorbet. Freeze completely and stir before serving.

Snapshots

Bzummar

The grapes, mainly Obedieh, Lebanon's indigenous Chardonnay-like grape, originally from Zahleh, and Cabernet Sauvignon from France, are grown in vineyards on the monastery's grounds. As is the case with most of Lebanon's monasteries, the wines were originally made for the monks' personal consumption at meal times and at religious services. Only recently, with the trickle of tourists and pilgrims who visit the often picturesque monasteries, have the monks started selling their produce.

Father Georges, one of the resident missionaries, tentatively explained the monastery's relationship with wine and the vine, as the stern, bearded faces of past bishops stared down from the walls of the main hall. 'Of course, before we were Christians, we were pagans. We had many gods and each was represented by a fruit. When we became Christians in 301 AD, we gave up all the fruit symbolism but kept the grape as a token vestige of that period. It represents both wine and of course the blood of Christ.'

Father Georges went on to explain that on *Eid Es Saydi* (the Feast of the Virgin Mary), on 15 August, the monastery blesses grapes brought by both local farmers hoping for a good crop as well as those grown by the monks and which are given away. 'We take this very seriously. No one eats the new grapes before the feast.'

Lebanese Varietals

The next time you open a bottle of Château Musar white wine, say the impressive '98, and taste the citrus, spice, wood, tobacco, butter and honey, remember that these fabulous notes come from Lebanon's indigenous Merweh and Obedieh grape varieties. The same grapes also go into making the best araks.

The taster may find it slightly harder to detect the hand of eighty-three-year-old Tanios Fahed (below), who grows grapes for Serge Hochar's famous label in the Mount Lebanon village of Beqaata in a vineyard first planted by his grandfather in 1872. (His father replanted in 1920 and Fahed planted his current vines in 1947.)

Lebanon's indigenous grapes are sorely under-used, and many of those, including Serge Hochar, who wish to champion them wonder why they are not used more in the making of arak and wine. However, although in the mid-nineteenth century the indigenous fruit was consumed by all the convents and the villagers, when the Lebanese wine industry began to expand at the time of the French mandate it was only normal that European influence would encourage Lebanese wine makers to import and use French vines.

Still, for those devotees of Lebanese grapes, the delight and wonder in what they give is that nothing much has changed in over 2,000 years. These are very, very old and simple grapes.

'From our original varietals, we cannot make sophisticated wines like the European *cépages*,' explains Jean Hage Chahine, arguably Lebanon's foremost authority on its indigenous grapes, 'but for centuries the people of Zahleh and the area have made arak and wine and when they had a bumper harvest and no space for the wine they would make *dibs* (molasses), which they could eat, and if not they could dilute it to make wine once more.'

Of the twenty-two indigenous varieties documented, he claims at least twenty will give good arak, but Obeideh and Souri will give the best, while Merweh, Obeideh, Mariami and possibly Sarini will give good wine.

'When I made my study I had to scour the country to find the twenty-two varietals. Sadly, little by little they have disappeared, maybe we only have six left. Have they gone? I don't know. It is very difficult to find them. There is little or no commercial culture and a few will have gone for ever.'

For ever? Does he mean they are extinct? Hage Chahine sighs. 'Maybe if you look really hard, you will find them. I have told the government it is their responsibility to do this. We should be classifying the ancient Lebanese varieties and trying to create new varieties from Lebanese vines. In France there are 150 varietals. Some come from Spain, Italy and Eastern Europe. They developed. They cross-bred. We must protect our grapes, as they are the basis of arak-making. We have a heritage. We were the first to develop these grapes. We have to look all over the country, even in Syria, in areas such as Homs and Aleppo. But we are protecting nothing. If we were, why have they all disappeared?'

The Zahleh way

The commercial arak industry began in Zahleh and nearby Qab Elias in the nineteenth century, when local priests taught the villagers how to make wine and then distil it into arak. Three families, the Toumas (who still make arak today and who also own Clos St Thomas and the Heritage wineries) and the Ghantous and Abou Raad families became synonymous with arak-making in the Zahleh area.

'Every Christmas, it was the tradition in Zahleh for each house in the town to receive a gallon jar of arak,' explains Selim Wardy, whose family owns the Domaine Wardy winery, which produces two commercial araks including the famous Ghantous, Abou Raad and Arak Wardy.

For committed drinkers it was accepted that they could buy on credit in winter on the condition that they pay for it with their summer wages. 'There was no work in winter and the only thing to do was to eat and sleep,' explains Wardy. 'Arak was a currency and a source of personal pride. It was OK to have no food in the house, but to have no arak was a badge of shame. It was the most important of the *mouni*.'

So steeped in the arak culture is Zahleh that there is a tale of how a local man, while drinking his daily glass of arak, might invoke God. 'With his first drink, he would call upon God and confess that he is a poor man who prays regularly. He asks God to look on the poor who toil in the fields all day and who feel that he often looks unkindly upon them,' explains Wardy. 'Then he has his second drink and becomes more impatient. He asks God where he is and why he does not listen to his complaints, before suggesting to God that he sit with him a while. With the third drink, he is more conciliatory, suggesting to God that they discuss his grievances like two grown men, but by the fourth drink God comes down and at last they talk. But by the fifth drink our man thinks he is God and scrambles to reach heaven. The next morning he prays for forgiveness until the next time, and so it continues.' Wardy smiles: 'This is the Zahleh way.'

Index